WHILE THEY WERE AT TABLE

Anna Burke is a Sister of Mercy who works in Pastoral Renewal in the diocese of Ardagh and Clonmacnois. She has worked in education and faith development in Florida, Zambia, South Africa and Ireland. Her particular interest is in praying with Scripture. Her previous publications include *Sacred the Hour: The Rosary Story in Mystery* (2007), *Where Blessings Flow: Words of Glory and Thanks* (2008), *When Silence Falls: The Stations of the Cross* (2008) and *In the Secret of My Heart: Moments of Stillness in the Heart of Christ* (2010), all published by Veritas.

WHILE THEY WERE AT TABLE

Eucharistic Prayers and Reflections

ANNA BURKE

VERITAS

Published 2012 by
Veritas Publications
7–8 Lower Abbey Street
Dublin 1, Ireland
publications@veritas.ie
www.veritas.ie

ISBN 978 1 84730 356 1
Copyright © Anna Burke, 2012

10 9 8 7 6 5 4 3 2 1

A catalogue record for this book is available from the
British Library.

Designed by Barbara Croatto, Veritas
Printed in the Republic of Ireland by Turner Printing Company Ltd,
Longford

Veritas books are printed on paper made from the wood pulp of
managed forests. For every tree felled, at least one tree is planted,
thereby renewing natural resources.

This book is dedicated to the givers and receivers, to those who work tirelessly to ease human hunger. It is especially dedicated to the Sisters of Mercy.

CONTENTS

INTRODUCTION   9

PART ONE: PRAYERS AT TABLE

WE GATHER   13
WE LISTEN   15
WE GIVE THANKS   17
WE OFFER GIFTS   19
WE SPEAK PEACE   21
WE BLESS   23
WE GO FORTH   25
WE ADORE   27

❖

PART TWO: STORIES AT TABLE

THE AWAKENING   31
THE LIVING MEMORY   37
THE REAL HUNGER   43
THE RESTING PLACE   51
THE HOLY HOUR   57
THE FOOD OF LIFE   63
THE COSMOS ON FIRE   69
THE DRINK OF WATER   75
THE SHARED GIFT   81
WHAT IS TRUTH?   87
THE ACCEPTANCE   93
THE ALTAR OF THE WORLD   99
A WOMAN OF THE EUCHARIST   105

Contents

PART ONE:

PART TWO:

INTRODUCTION

IT IS ALWAYS THE right time to stop in amazement before the love that stayed beyond rejection and death. Jesus, who had found his birthplace on the earth, bound himself to us in a relationship that was invincible. Leaving us was unthinkable at this level of love. He would remain forever on the table of the world.

In his encyclical of 22 February 2007, *Sacramentum Caritatis*, Pope Benedict XVI calls us to find relief for our hunger in 'the food of truth'. The Pope, in continuity with his first encyclical *Deus Caritas Est* and revisiting the thoughts of his predecessor John Paul II's *Ecclesia de Eucharistia*, invites us into the sacrificial meal, from where we draw our very life. Pope Benedict asks all people to draw near to God's love because it holds the deepest desire of the human heart.

In this book, the author ponders some of the images and metaphors from *Sacramentum Caritatis* in particular, and offers her reflections and prayers as a resource for personal and communal meditation and contemplation.

Part One: Prayers At Table leads us on a journey through the Mass. The prayers focus on the various liturgical moments of the sacred rite and help to heighten our awareness of the communion of all creation in the Sacred Mystery. These 'Prayers At Table' offer a valuable resource for catechesis on the Mass, prayers of intercession, times of prayer with Eucharistic theme, and private prayer.

Part Two: Stories At Table helps us to explore some key texts from Scripture which direct us to the table of communion. These reflections, inspired by Pope Benedict XVI, together with 'Homily Thoughts', provide significant material for assistance in a variety of situations, including praying with Scripture, Eucharistic prayer, times of reflection in Mass, prayer groups and Eucharistic adoration.

When faith stumbles we find our reason at the table where he handed over his life.

When hope wavers we find our anchor at the table where he is always present.

When love fails we find our restoration at the table where he offers us the Bread of Life.

PART ONE

PRAYERS AT TABLE

PART ONE

WE GATHER

God is here, keeping pace with us, welcoming us. We gather in friendship.
Every knee shall bow, every tongue confess that Jesus Christ is Lord.

God is here, in every heartbeat, in every anxiety, in every breath. We gather in faith.
Every knee shall bow, every tongue confess that Jesus Christ is Lord.

God is here, in every man, woman and child, in every personality, in every struggle. We gather in reverence.
Every knee shall bow, every tongue confess that Jesus Christ is Lord.

God is here, in every misunderstanding, in every stress, in every regret, in every broken effort. We gather in reconciliation.
Every knee shall bow, every tongue confess that Jesus Christ is Lord.

God is here, in the Eucharist, in the Bread of Life, in the flesh of Jesus. God is truly here. We gather in thanksgiving.
Every knee shall bow, every tongue confess that Jesus Christ is Lord.

God is here, in every prayer, in every sigh, in every song, in every silence. We gather in worship.
Every knee shall bow, every tongue confess that Jesus Christ is Lord.

We Listen

O God, I am listening. I desire a sacred dialogue with you that I may hear the call of deep relationship.
Let me hear your voice, O God.

O God, I am listening. I hear the story that connects human history, from Egypt to Jerusalem to the ends of the earth. May I be a bond of connection in this story.
Let me hear your voice, O God.

O God, I am listening. I acclaim the saving action of God through the Word, Jesus Christ. May I be a herald of this news across the fields of my journey.
Let me hear your voice, O God.

O God, I am listening. I feel my heart burning within me at the sound of your voice. May I come to recognise the distinguishable quality of your voice wherever and whenever it speaks to me.
Let me hear your voice, O God.

O God, I am listening. I am deeply affected by the words of mercy that come from your mouth. May my listening give me the ability to distinguish voices and to know the caller.
Let me hear your voice, O God.

O God, I am listening. I am open to the influence of the Word who has power to provide bread for the whole world. May I be transformed by this Word and become a giver of bread.

Let me hear your voice, O God.

O God, I am listening. I receive on my table the Bread of your Word. With Mary, I understand how this Word is the hope of our time, the river in the desert and I ask Mary to help me also to be a Christ-bearer.

Let me hear your voice, O God.

WE GIVE THANKS

At the dawning of each day we give you thanks O God, for the victory of light, for new beginnings.
I thank you forever, my Lord and my God.

At the morning hour we give you thanks O God, for parents and grandparents, teachers and guardians who directed our first steps and our first words to your love and protection.
I thank you forever, my Lord and my God.

At the evening of our lives in the setting of the sun we give you thanks O God, for the miles we walked together.
I thank you forever, my Lord and my God.

At the moment of opportunity in the vision of the dream we give you thanks O God, for the colours, shapes, sounds and smells that awaken our senses to life.
I thank you forever, my Lord and my God.

At the ninth hour when fear and sickness bring down the night, we give you thanks O God, for carrying us through the darkness.
I thank you forever, my Lord and my God.

At the season of joy and celebration we give you thanks O God, for health and happiness and laughter and song.
I thank you forever, my Lord and my God.

At the times of achievement and victory we give you thanks O God, for good health, creative skill and perseverance.
I thank you forever, my Lord and my God.

At the hour of death and departure we give you thanks O God, for the journey accomplished, for the promise of going on.
I thank you forever, my Lord and my God.

At every step of life's journey we give you thanks, O God, for family, friends, neighbours and workmates, who light our way with friendship and hope.
I thank you forever, my Lord and my God.

WE OFFER GIFTS

We offer the gift of our food, given to us for eating and for sharing. May it be a sign of our unity with all people who hunger for the Bread of Life.
Receive our gifts O God, for the glory of your name.

We offer the gift of our speech, given to us to tell of the wonders of God. May it become part of the great voice of the assembly, gathered at the table to worship and to serve.
Receive our gifts O God, for the glory of your name.

We offer the gift of our material goods, given to us for responsible stewardship, to serve the cause of human dignity and peace on earth. May these gifts of shared resources, be a sign of our communion in the Body of Christ, who gathers all people at the Table of the World.
Receive our gifts O God, for the glory of your name.

We offer the gift of our faith, given to us from the heart of God, that we might build our lives in Christ and come to know the height and depth of God's love. May our faith be a signpost on the road.
Receive our gifts O God, for the glory of your name.

We offer the gift of our hope, given to us that we might survive the darkest hour and keep the lamp burning. May our hope keep us trusting in the wisdom of God for answers, and in the dream of God for fulfilment.
Receive our gifts O God, for the glory of your name.

We offer the gift of our love, given to us that we might be fully alive with the passion of Christ, for giving and forgiving, for breaking the bread and sharing the cup. May our love be part of the great and ultimate love of God, born in time, offered on the altar, available in the meal.
Receive our gifts O God, for the glory of your name.

WE SPEAK PEACE

Peace to all people of good will, who think with understanding and send out a blessing.
Blessed are the peacemakers; they shall see God.

Peace to all people of good will, who pour dew drops on frozen soil and cause the sun to come out.
Blessed are the peacemakers; they shall see God.

Peace to all people of good will, who go to meet the enemy and open the bridge of hope.
Blessed are the peacemakers; they shall see God.

Peace to all people of good will, who close the chapter on suspicion and separation and extend the hand of friendship.
Blessed are the peacemakers; they shall see God.

Peace to all people of good will, who acknowledge their own blindness and break ranks to stop the cycle of violence.
Blessed are the peacemakers; they shall see God.

Peace to all people of good will, who offer their lives in the service of others, as peaceshapers and peacemakers, as peaceseekers and peacekeepers.
Blessed are the peacemakers; they shall see God.

Peace to all people of good will, who share their material and spiritual resources on the altar of the world.
Blessed are the peacemakers; they shall see God.

Peace to all people of good will, who replace the harsh word with the kind word, who respond to criticism with understanding, whose spirits are enlarged by love.
Blessed are the peacemakers; they shall see God.

Peace to all people of good will, who make contact, and dig tunnels and keep the candle lighting and offer the cup of tea. Peace to them for where they reside, God lives.
Blessed are the peacemakers; they shall see God.

WE BLESS

PRIEST: I bless you with the love of Christ. May his love carry you safely all your days.

ALL: Christ be within me, Christ be below me, Christ be above me, never to part.

PRIEST: I bless you with the peace of Christ. May his peace relieve the pain and anxiety that is in your hearts.

ALL: Christ be within me, Christ be below me, Christ be above me, never to part.

PRIEST: I bless you with the presence of Christ. May his presence be beside you, within you, before you, always.

ALL: Christ be within me, Christ be below me, Christ be above me, never to part.

PRIEST: I bless you with the healing of Christ. May his healing fill you and restore you.

ALL: Christ be within me, Christ be below me, Christ be above me, never to part.

PRIEST: I bless you with the forgiveness of Christ. May his forgiveness magnify your vision and inspire your decisions.

ALL: Christ be within me, Christ be below me, Christ be above me, never to part.

PRIEST: I bless you with the faithfulness of Christ. May his faithfulness deepen your friendships and strengthen your relationships.

ALL: Christ be within me, Christ be below me, Christ be above me, never to part.

PRIEST: I bless you with the Body of Christ. May the Eucharist be the source and summit of your journey back to God.

ALL: Christ be within me, Christ be below me, Christ be above me, never to part.

We Go Forth

Christ of the journey lead us out of this place for we are nourished for the road ahead, confident and unafraid.
May we go forth with Christ.

Christ of the server, guide us as we seek out the forgotten people, for we are nourished for the mission field, our eyes opened with compassion.
May we go forth with Christ.

Christ of the traveller, stay with us as we leave Jerusalem, filled with the memory, carrying the towel and basin, our feet ready for the extra mile.
May we go forth with Christ.

Christ of the healer, walk with us into the places of sorrow, for we are nourished for the night watch, our hands anointed with reconciliation.
May we go forth with Christ.

Christ of the speaker, give us the words of eternal life, for we are nourished for the proclamation, our voices alive with the Good News that Jesus Christ has saved us.
May we go forth with Christ.

Christ of the captive, direct our search for prison doors, for we are nourished with the freedom call, our hearts telling of the amnesty, that we may open the snares and let the people go free.

May we go forth with Christ.

WE ADORE

Blessed be God
Blessed be the holy name of God
Blessed be the sacred universe that God created
Blessed be the life systems that reflect the glory of God
Blessed be Jesus the divine son, true God and true man
Blessed be the name of Jesus
Blessed be the heart of Jesus, burning with love for us
Blessed be the face of God in Jesus
Blessed be the Holy Spirit, who pleads our cause
Blessed be the Holy Spirit, who guides us in holiness
Blessed be the Holy Spirit, fire and energy of God
Blessed be Mary, Mother of God
Blessed be Mary, Queen of heaven and earth
Blessed be Joseph, spouse of Mary
Blessed be Joseph, just and humble man
Blessed be all the angels and saints of God, on earth and
    in heaven
Blessed be all who speak of God's love
Blessed be all who long to see God
Blessed be the holy communion of people who praise God.

PART TWO

STORIES AT TABLE

THE AWAKENING
LUKE 24:13-35

'NOW ON THAT SAME DAY TWO OF THEM WERE GOING TO A VILLAGE CALLED EMMAUS, ABOUT SEVEN MILES FROM JERUSALEM, AND TALKING WITH EACH OTHER ABOUT ALL THESE THINGS THAT HAD HAPPENED.' It was another journey taken in sadness, two people walking away from the memory of loss. They may have believed that extra miles would separate them from the pain and bewilderment of suffering, and so they kept moving away from the place of memories, running for refuge, hoping for escape. Emmaus offered the absence of distant places and on this same day when news of an empty tomb was spreading through the countryside, two grieving hearts kept walking.

'WHILE THEY WERE TALKING AND DISCUSSING, JESUS HIMSELF CAME NEAR AND WENT WITH THEM, BUT THEIR EYES WERE KEPT FROM RECOGNISING HIM.' It was a journey of aloneness – perspective blurred and awareness choked. They saw him but they were searching for a memory; he walked along with them but they were unable for companionship. Jesus broke into their empty world that day and asked to be admitted to their company. He had caught up with them in the escape and he would be there when the shadows lengthened and the day closed down.

'Are you the only stranger in Jerusalem who does not know the things that have taken place there in these days?' Cleopas was frustrated with the man who was unbroken by the event in Jerusalem. Is it possible that someone could have survived

Jerusalem? Perhaps he was a stranger who had come in for Passover and didn't understand the language of Rome. Maybe he wanted to hear the other side, to put the record straight, to refocus the story. It was just possible, Cleopas thought, that the man who didn't know about Golgotha knew something about Jesus.

'What things?' The very question, though puzzling, was a relief, an avenue into release, an opening of the emotional safe. They told him everything. They included details of the dead man's lineage, of his prophetic quality and of the expectation he created in human history and in human hearts. They emphasised how he was a continuity figure, a sign of God's faithfulness to the promise, a man with the power of love. Oddly enough, as they explained to their companion, it was these very qualities that sent shock waves through the established order and brought down the wrath of the justice system. The people who had hoped that he would set Israel free were dismayed at his failure, but those who sensed the immensity of his power were happy to have silenced him – forever!

'Some women of our group astounded us. They were at the tomb early in the morning and when they did not find his body there, they came back and told them that they had indeed seen a vision of angels who said that he was alive.' Although this was a turning point in the story, the two on the road to Emmaus didn't seem to put the pieces together. The testimony of the women broke into the darkness as dawn follows night and their witness of the empty tomb, though subject to confirmation, changed the genre of the story. This compelling evidence was set to light up the Emmaus journey and all journeys leading from it.

'He explained to them what was said about him in all the Scriptures.' The stranger is now moving more visibly into the story, into their footsteps. He returns the conversation to its context and situates all that has happened within the definitive plan of God. The journey to Emmaus becomes a movement into discovery, a pathway of stepping stones revealing the direction. The sorrow has eased now and the dialogue has deepened. There is the recall of Moses, who escaped the folly of Egypt, and the prophets who liberated the trap of history with their lives. The strands are weaving a lifeline, forming a unity of threads, bringing the encounter to its fulfilment.

'THEY URGED HIM STRONGLY, SAYING, "STAY WITH US BECAUSE IT IS ALMOST EVENING AND THE DAY IS NOW NEARLY OVER." SO HE WENT IN TO STAY WITH THEM.' This is what they were searching for, their reason for departing Jerusalem. The empty space was intolerable and so they had set out, searching. When evening closed in there was a strange fire in the sunset and the silence began to listen and their hearts trembled with a burning desire. 'Stay with us,' they pleaded, now that the evening star is rising over the village and the air is full of mystery and the distance has come to rest. 'Stay with us,' they prayed, for your walking with us has torn the veil from our eyes and intensified our longing for food. So he went in to stay with them.

'WHEN HE WAS AT TABLE WITH THEM, HE TOOK BREAD, BLESSED AND BROKE IT AND GAVE IT TO THEM. THEN THEIR EYES WERE OPENED, AND THEY RECOGNISED HIM.' It was a long journey from letting go to finding again, from desperation to serenity. The two people who had left Jerusalem in the morning of that day believed that Golgotha was an end point, a conclusion in failure. They had departed Jerusalem to find another starting place and perhaps to forget. However, while they were at table the memory took a human shape and the journey became a gateway to the meeting place. They knew the familiar gestures, the blessing and the breaking, the giving and the sharing; and while they were at table they remembered the promise. Emmaus was now the place of encounter.

Homily Thoughts

❊ The journey away from loss sometimes takes us out of
Jerusalem, from the very place where God set us free.
It is difficult to recognise God on the rough miles and
direction becomes an issue.

❊ The journey has a learning time. Jesus goes with us to be
there at the turning of the tide. Life is about putting the
pieces together, seeing the whole context, discovering the
bigger plan, finding a new perspective.

❊ The journey has a remembering time, when telling the
story helps us to connect the chapters and to see the plan
on the map of our lives. It is the Word of God that sustains
us when the direction is unclear.

❊ The journey has a breakthrough time. It was late in the
afternoon for the disciples. Sometimes discovery takes a
lifetime. It came for the disciples when they invited him
in, opened their home in hospitality, welcomed him to
table. The breakthrough was the moment of Eucharist.

❊ The journey to Emmaus is the journey of transformation.
As they listened on the road to the Word, their hearts
began to burn with the presence of fire.

❊ The journey is the road into discovery. At the end of
the journey we shall see and taste the banquet. They
recognised him in the breaking of the bread.

THE TRUTH OF LOVE

> Jesus shows us how the truth of love can transform even the dark mystery of death into the radiant light of the resurrection. Here the splendour of God's glory surpasses all worldly beauty.
>
> Benedict XVI, *Sacramentum Caritatis*, 35

It was a day like all the other days and perfect for fishing. The three men were lifelong companions, skilled in their art, comfortable at sea. They had set out in the evening light hoping for a catch. As the old trawler headed for open waters a numbing sound engulfed the engine and with a deathlike tremor, the vessel started to capsize beneath the sleeping waters. It happened quickly and in the struggle for survival the men got separated. The skipper who remembered to release the life raft was tragically dragged under by the tangled debris. The others shouted to him to save himself but as darkness covered the hillsides, he was gone. They who had loved him watched him die.

The news of the fishing disaster spread through the neighbourhood and the community stood in silence, and waited. When the skipper's body was recovered the search for the remaining two men gathered pace. They might possibly have made it to the cave? Perhaps they were still holding on, somewhere? The cave on the offshore island had come to be associated with disorientation and lost travellers. It was a last beacon of hope in every search, and cave stories were the stuff of mystery and courage. The cave, though dark and perilous, held the secrets of survival and immortalised the thirst for life.

The men were found alive. The raft had carried them safely to the cave. As they remembered the journey they spoke about the loss of light and their bewilderment as they watched their colleague die. Revisiting the moments that brought them to their day of rescue, the survivors recalled how they wrestled with the temptation to give up and prayed for an escape route from the wreckage of death. As hunger pressed in on them and the walls around them became a tomb, someone shone a torch into the mouth of the cave.

Let Us Pray

Blessed be God.
Blessed be the holy name of God.
Blessed be the companionship of God on the road.
Blessed be the conversation of God in the silence.
Blessed be the wisdom of God in the confusion.
Blessed be the Word of God in the story.
Blessed be the cave of God in the struggle.
Blessed be the light of God in the darkness.
Blessed be the faithfulness of God in the ending.
Blessed be the continuity of God in the death.
Blessed be the village of God in the evening.
Blessed be the table of God in the gathering.
Blessed be the bread of God in the mealtime.
Blessed be the family of God in the communion.

THE LIVING MEMORY
LUKE 22:14-20

'WHEN THE HOUR CAME HE TOOK HIS PLACE AT TABLE.'
As Luke draws all time into this hour, there is
anticipation and there is history in the room. All creation has
been waiting for this moment, foretold from the beginning. It
is the hour of the first light, the hour of redemption. The air
is fixed with expectation as Passover stories are retold and the
day of release is remembered.

He had lived for this communion, but as he sat down to
table he knew where love would lead him. Gathered with his
friends in this critical hour, he knew that he had accomplished
his essential task, to seek and to find, to gather and to feed.
The table was his vineyard, a sign of the family man, the one
who gives his life. At the table he would continue to serve, to
restore hearts that are broken, to renew spirits that are shut
down. The broken bread would become his unbroken bond.

'I HAVE EAGERLY DESIRED TO EAT THIS PASSOVER WITH
YOU BEFORE I SUFFER.' His very life was born of this desire,
to be the heart of our communion, the living memory. Love
is always above the ordinary. He wanted to accomplish our
liberation, to see us safely across the finish line, to be there at
the handing over, whatever it cost. Love is always above the
earnings. He wanted to take to himself every mistake, every
shortfall, every broken promise, just as mothers and fathers
do. He would wipe the slate clean, again, and pay our debts.
Love is always above reason. It was the hour of pouring out,
of the killing of the Lamb; it was the hour of forgiving the

prodigal child, of embracing the criminal. He eagerly desired to be there for us until we reached the land.

'THEN HE TOOK A LOAF OF BREAD, AND WHEN HE HAD GIVEN THANKS, HE BROKE IT AND GAVE IT TO THEM, SAYING, "THIS IS MY BODY, WHICH IS GIVEN FOR YOU. DO THIS IN REMEMBRANCE OF ME."' The bread and wine are part of us; we planted the seeds, nurtured them and brought them to the table. Wheat and grapes have a particularly human content for they are woven into our tales of war and peace, of feasts and famines, of struggles and achievements. The bread and wine are a global connection, at the table of kings and in the smallest kitchen. They unite us in our hunger and remind us in our excess. When he took the bread and wine he lifted up the earth community, out of the dust, into his heart. It was the gesture that signalled abundance, generosity and restoration. The hour of transformation was here, and we were all called to the banquet, to become the Bread. The familiar words which previously announced the feeding of thousands were heard again at the table in Jerusalem. We hear once more the gathering of the multitudes, the ending of hunger and the possibility of the shared bread. The table time is now the memory for our journey, when the bread became the food of eternal life.

'TAKE THIS AND DIVIDE IT AMONG YOURSELVES; FOR THIS IS MY BODY.' Jesus presents his very life as food for the world. The focus at table turns to the source of the food, to the bread of nations. It is given to be divided and distributed and shared so that all may be one at the meal. The words of giving have all the marks of abandonment, nothing will be withheld, nothing calculated. The love at the table is always about us, it will lay down its life to save us.

This is his body, broken for the cause, given for the people, to keep them together, to nurture them in the desert crossing, to bring them to the table of communion. This is his body, born in historical time, reaching beyond all time. This is his body, passing over to life, holding the imprint of the victory. 'Do this in remembrance of me': gather the people and come to my table. Bring all who are hungry and thirsting for life. Call them from the byways and alleyways. Make an extra space for the latecomer. Do not spare the bread. Finish the wine. Form the great communion of heaven and earth. Welcome the stray; give your chair to the fallen. Let the great transformation begin with you and among you until the war is over. Eat together from the Bread of Life and share the place of friendship - and when you do, do it in memory of me.

HOMILY THOUGHTS

❋ The occasion of a meal marks Jesus' passing-over time. This is a threshold moment for all creation. With Jesus we will all pass over death, into freedom.

❋ We all mark threshold times with the sharing of meals. It's a way of saying that our common identity is unshakable, that our bond of friendship unites us across time and place.

❋ The occasion of a meal marks a transfiguration time. The mountain of Tabor prepared us for this meal. On the mountain we beheld the glory of God in the body of Jesus. The memory of Tabor helps us to understand the new form of presence that Jesus will have with us. This passing-over meal is a moment of transfiguration, when the bread and wine reveal the glory of God.

❋ The link has now been made between the sacrificed Lamb, the shared meal and the transformation of the human body. We who gather at his table are participants in the covenant, partners in the mission for the passing over of creation to God.

❦ The occasion of the meal is a resurrection time. The physical reality has a new substance. The body and blood become living food and life beyond the tomb becomes the new reality.

❦ The occasion of this meal is a remembering time: 'Do this in remembrance of me.' We are commissioned to gather in love at the table, to share the bread and to become the body that transforms the world.

❦ Remembering is a Christian responsibility, the action that says we are passing over with Christ, a people set free. Remembering is a promise fulfilled, a covenant kept.

The Stones Remember

> Every great reform has in some way been linked to the rediscovery of belief in the Lord's eucharistic presence among his people.
>
> *Sacramentum Caritatis*, 6

The entrance sign at Ballintubber Abbey, Co. Mayo, welcomes us to a place of 'enduring hope' and of 'faithful love'. We are reminded that we stand on holy ground, for this is the dwelling place of a people who have gathered at the table of the Eucharist since 1216. Their story is one of survival, courage and worship. Through fires, persecutions and attacks from every side, against the orders of kings and the ravages of famine, the Abbey of the Holy Trinity refused to be silenced.

When the Penal Laws brought Ireland to its knees, and with it Ballintubber Abbey, the people gathered in their roofless church to celebrate Mass. Today, on the abbey grounds, the graves of those who divided the Bread of Life and ate it, now face the rising sun.

The green fields form a setting of great serenity at Ballintubber Abbey and the sheep are still with good grazing, trusting the shepherd to protect their vulnerability. There is a small bridge crossing the stream, giving a sense of entering in. This is one of those unique places where stories of druidic ritual and Christian worship find their common source at the ancient well, on the chariot route, at the mountain top.

There is a timeless landscape here. The well, now known as St Patrick's Well, is a river of life in this 'the town of the well'. It has never been known to run dry and is remembered today as the place of welcome where Patrick baptised the people who longed for living water. From the abbey, Patrick took the long ancient chariot route to Cruachan Aigle, the sacred mountain of our pre-Christian ancestors, thereby marking it as the pilgrim way. Tochar Phadraig has, over the centuries, merged into the identity of all who walk the miles over stones and hills, through ditches and valleys, yearning for communion with God and with one another. The Pilgrim Route is truly a eucharistic experience, marked by moments of thanksgiving, inclusion, light and communion.

The local community still comes to the abbey to worship and visitors are drawn irresistibly into the history of a remembering people. Windows from the thirteenth century and a doorway from the fifteenth century, together with natural stone features, capture the wonder of a history where God visited his people and set them free. In 2016, Ballintubber Abbey will celebrate 800 years of life, an occasion for all of us to leave the main Castlebar–Galway road and gather at the table that we may 'Do this in memory'.

Let Us Pray

Blessed be God.
Blessed be the holy name of God.
Blessed be the creative energy of God.
Blessed be the stones in the hands of God.
Blessed be the people in the plan of God.
Blessed be the hope in the vision of God.
Blessed be the patience in the way of God.
Blessed be the abbey in the path of God.
Blessed be the awakening in the field of God.
Blessed be the purpose in the mind of God.
Blessed be the transformation in the heart of God.
Blessed be the table in the house of God.
Blessed be the history in the writing of God.

THE REAL HUNGER
LUKE 9:10-17

'BUT THE CROWDS LEARNED ABOUT IT AND FOLLOWED HIM. HE WELCOMED THEM AND SPOKE TO THEM ABOUT THE KINGDOM OF GOD ... ' We all follow the hope and pursue the promise of life. There were stories of healing in the countryside at the time and these awakened intense human desire. The possibility of someone who could bring back the life in us was magnetic. We would be able to sit beside him and touch him and eat with him. This was the kind of religion that they longed for, an experience of real presence. No one could keep the people from Jesus that day. They had heard of his power to take away hunger and they set out to find him. They needed the human encounter, the physical reality and they found him in Bethsaida. Although he was on his break after a day in the field, he welcomed the extended family and seeing the hope in their eyes he healed those who needed healing. They learned that day that Jesus is never beyond our reach, the one who never signs out.

'SEND THE CROWD AWAY, SO THAT THEY CAN GO TO THE SURROUNDING VILLAGES AND COUNTRYSIDE, AND FIND FOOD AND LODGING ... ' The disciples felt that it was time to close down for the day. This was how the system worked and the people would have to provide for themselves in the 'after hours'. Surely discipleship could not be used as an umbrella for every social need, and having preached the Word by day, the disciples of Jesus believed that responsibility for evening meals resided with someone else. There was the additional issue of numbers and they simply did not have the skills to address hunger at crisis level. The disciples' final argument was their shortage of food. Jesus understood very well that food was indeed the focus of the gathering, the reason the people had followed him, and so he invited them to table. It was a communion lesson for the disciples, the purpose and goal of their ministry.

'YOU GIVE THEM SOMETHING TO EAT.' Sending the people away is not an option. The problem is ours, to be owned and to be addressed. The disciples of Jesus must discover where the food of life is stored and lead the people to the meal. It is their responsibility to make the food available for the common good, for the relief of hunger. The words of Jesus are the material of revolutions! There is a trembling in the social order as the banquet of the nations begins. Discipleship is the job of being my brother's keeper, of breaking the bread that others may eat. It is the art of inclusiveness and the service of all humanity, on the table of the world. The command of Jesus is in the nature of a new radical awareness that all are called to the banquet, that all have a right to the food.

'WE HAVE ONLY FIVE LOAVES OF BREAD AND TWO FISH – UNLESS WE GO AND BUY FOOD FOR ALL THE CROWD.' What is it about resources? We never seem to have enough! There is the ceaseless cry for more investment capital and more bond shares, for additional capacity and for things made of gold. Material solutions have always been inadequate – in Bethsaida and in our capital cities – because their addictive nature has the effect of aggravating hunger. The disciples in the story who are grappling with shortage problems will have to find an alternate source. Human hunger, they will learn, is not insurmountable. The solution, however, will require new understandings of root causes and of sustainable remedies. The feeding of the multitude will have to be addressed in terms of the civilisation of love.

'HAVE THEM SIT DOWN IN GROUPS OF ABOUT FIFTY EACH.' As the people take their places, a new definition of crisis management becomes apparent. It is based on making space for everyone at the table of the world, of including everyone in the gathering. The disciples must learn to listen to the voice of the people; they must make sure that the bread is shared. This new social consciousness will stir the winds of transformation until civilisation is understood. Jesus has put the focus here on the one who holds the key to the cupboard. As he gathered the people that day, he was about to reveal that resources are sufficient when they are shared. Jesus is asking us in every generation, 'How many loaves do you have?'

'TAKING THE FIVE LOAVES AND THE TWO FISH, HE LOOKED UP TO HEAVEN, HE GAVE THANKS AND BROKE THEM. THEN HE GAVE THEM TO THE DISCIPLES TO DISTRIBUTE TO THE PEOPLE.' Jesus does not dismiss their limited resources but he releases them. We have as much as we are prepared to give, for giving increases life expectancy. Jesus is obviously pushing out the boundaries on our interpretation, asking us to recheck our resources for the sake of the hungry multitude. In releasing our bread for others, we release Christ on the world with his measureless source of compassion. The link between Christ and the alleviation of hunger is inescapable for the disciples. A life-giving nutrition centre always includes the Bread of Life. When Jesus asked his disciples to distribute the loaves and fish he called them to the ministry of shared resources, to the dream of communion.

'THEY ALL ATE AND WERE FILLED.' From this moment, there is a change in our understanding of the source of food. The disciples of Jesus are no longer relying on counting loaves and fish because a resource of infinite magnitude is available to them, and from this source all people will be fed. No contribution is too small to make a difference and Jesus reveals to us how resources grow in the giving. When we release the little we have, we bring about the transformation of society.

As the baskets are returned, we know that something has begun that will not be depleted. Jesus has spread a wonderful feast, an abundant table, for all the people. The moment is universal, the bread is the love of a person for his people. Jesus can feed the world.

Homily Thoughts

❧ Where there is hope the people gather. We all flock to the places that offer even the slightest chance of touching God. The human heart gravitates to any person, place or thing that offers an encounter with the divine. We are willing to pay any price for the experience and so we climb mountains, pray through the night, fast and go barefooted, just for the tiniest glimpse, a single moment of awareness, of hope.

❧ Where there is hope there is God. Jesus is not asking for a price; he is giving everything he has. The camera is not on our efforts but on the generosity of God. This is the heart of Eucharist. He is awaiting our arrival with abundant hospitality. We do not have to earn his love; he has prepared a table for us.

❧ Where there is hope, hunger is eased and longing is satisfied. The loaves and fish are a promise of God's compassionate care for us, of a love that knows no ending.

❧ Where there is hope there are people who gather in love to care and to share, to receive the Bread and to take it to the world. Hope is not silenced by poverty; it has always more to give.

THE CIVILISATION OF LOVE

> The Food of truth demands that we denounce inhumane situations in which people starve to death because of injustice and exploitation, and it gives us renewed strength and courage to work tirelessly in the service of the civilisation of love.
>
> *Sacramentum Caritatis*, 90

Society was changing and gone were the days of oppressive institutions, as cultural liberation opened new windows of opportunity. All that remained was to rid the earth of dictatorships and to make room for new forms of global collusion. This, the people were told, would ensure the humanisation of systems and the enrichment of cultures. People would be enabled to live together and decide for the common good. Someone suggested that love might be the language of the new corporation, replacing ethnic confusion with a more harmonious communication. It was thought to be too subversive, however, as it threatened to reveal the depths of the human dimension and perhaps to inaugurate a period of common ownership.

The debate raged at the highest levels. It was the possibility of people beginning to think for themselves and refusing to be the agents of economic empires and property vultures that threatened the new global phenomenon. One of the international political analysts thought that love was actually a pernicious force with potential to attack privatisation, release imprisoned minds and to demand a share of the harvest. It was finally ruled out on the basis of the collapse of the social edifice and the emergence of voices.

The people persisted, however, and took their dream to the streets. Their neighbours took up the cry and the demand for change grew and became a sacred duty. There was a new awareness everywhere and people began speaking a common language and the shouting lowered its volume to silence. As more and more people put down their weapons in the name of civilisation, the international expression changed. This led to a changed experience and finally the global power structure began to tremble.

The seats of power were shaken with the impact of the new language and they began to change position. Someone identified the peaceful uprising as a hunger for the civilisation of love. Slowly, the powers of states began to see that their own language would have to change if there was to be continued progress in the global movement. Somehow they would have to listen to the voice of the people who were convinced that the quality of a society was determined by the love people had for one another.

The demand for a seismic shift in the international debate intensified. The people roared against economic oppression, its squalor and degradation, its evil unfairness. The DNA altering took some time, but gradually the markets opened their boundary walls and the shares were distributed at the stalls.

The new civilisation of love took justice beyond equity and called it friendship; beyond giving and called it receiving; beyond decency and called it affection; beyond treaties and called it forgiveness; beyond race and called it family. The global empire itself began to speak of a new era for all creation.

LET US PRAY

Blessed be God.
Blessed be the holy name of God.
Blessed be the compassion of God.
Blessed be the hospitality of God's house.
Blessed be the welcome of God's voice.
Blessed be the abundance of God's mercy.
Blessed be the civilising power of God's love.
Blessed be the warmth of God's table.
Blessed be the gift of God's food.
Blessed be Jesus, the bread of God's life.
Blessed be Jesus, the well of God's renewal.
Blessed be Jesus, the Lamb of God's banquet.

THE RESTING PLACE
MATTHEW 12:1-8

'AT THAT TIME, JESUS WENT THROUGH THE CORNFIELDS ON THE SABBATH; HIS DISCIPLES WERE HUNGRY AND THEY BEGAN TO PLUCK HEADS OF GRAIN TO EAT.' Without delay this Sabbath story leads us into the imagery of hunger and food, of fatigue and desire. The walkers need restoration and they reach for the bread of life. It is a simple action, another chapter in the human search for the Sabbath rest. The presence of Jesus in the cornfield on the Sabbath day reminds us that he who was with God in the beginning is now at the heart of Sabbath. The memory of creation rest and of deliverance from Egypt come alive in the cornfield and with Jesus this memory takes on a new intensity.

'WHEN THE PHARISEES SAW IT, THEY SAID TO HIM, "LOOK, YOUR DISCIPLES ARE DOING WHAT IS NOT LAWFUL TO DO ON THE SABBATH."' The intervention of the Pharisees has the darkness of a witch hunt and the limitation of interpretation. They are revealing to us the effects of imprisonment of the mind, for both the purpose of their vigilance and the blindness of their scholarship are now in question. Interpretation has a way of yielding to distortion and of implicating others in its findings. The Pharisees have failed the Law and the Law has been used as a tool of investigative power. At this point in the Scripture, the need to find a new reference point for the ancient Law is urgent. The Sabbath day offers the hope that the new Law will free us from the tension and anxiety of conformity, that we may become alive.

'Have you not read what David did when he and his companions were hungry? He entered the house of God and ate the bread of Presence, which it was not lawful for him or his companions to eat ... ' Have you not read that the story of God with us is one of restoration? Have you not read how ancient Israel was fed the bread from heaven when the people hungered for the land? Have you not read how your ancestors left the grapes in the fields for the wanderer? Have you not read how the Sabbath festival was the sign of Israel's crossing over, of the victory of Abraham's God, of the covenant relationship? Have you not read? The Sabbath Law cannot be understood apart from the mercy of God. Sabbath ritual is meaningless if it disregards the human need to break out of the endless cycle of time and find rest in the timeless zone of God's love. Worship and charity are inseparable, for God is the meeting place of the vertical and horizontal, the place of eternal rest.

'I tell you something greater than the temple is here.' The story is redirected; the Law is revealed in its integrity. The Sabbath moment now stands at a threshold where it is reflected in the Jesus event. The ancient temple will return to stone, for something greater is here and all creation has found its entrance to the Sabbath rest.

Jesus reaches back to the prophet Hosea to show us that God's Law is a gift of freedom, conceived in mercy, written in the blood poured out. The Sabbath observance for Israel and for us has the common link of sacred covenant, the engagement of a people with their God, in delight and in faithfulness. God did not design Law for occupational therapy, his nor ours. It was a decision to liberate, to set free the slave and the householder, the ox and the ass. The Sabbath rest was a time to remember how God broke the cycle of work and rested all creation from servitude. It was that special time to celebrate God, whose goodness and compassion defeated the bonds of time. God's Law has the single purpose of fulfilling our destiny and leading us to the cornfield.

'For the Son of Man is lord of the Sabbath.' This is what the conflict was really about: the identity of Jesus. He is Lord of the Sabbath and within his redemptive action the Law has its quality and purpose. The camera of the Pharisees is too technical, too dependent on standing still; they will need a different lens to get to the root of the story. A continued interpretation of the Law without reference to Christ is ignorance of Scripture, for a new temple has risen from the ashes. Every Sabbath forevermore is about the identity of Jesus, the Lord of the Sabbath.

Homily Thoughts

❧ The Sabbath day points to our resting place with God. It is an acknowledgement that creation, life, achievement, productivity all belong to God. To keep the Sabbath is to acknowledge God's presence with us.

❧ The Sabbath day is a gift. It is the gift of freedom from the bondage of slavery, in its many forms. The earth itself and all that live on the earth are groaning to be set free. When work becomes an idol, it becomes a ceaseless toil and a violence to all living things. When work becomes the preeminent force on life's journey, all relationships are threatened. Sabbath day is not about laws; it is an exodus to freedom. God has visited us and set us free.

❧ The Sabbath day is a human right. Sabbath promotes us in our desire to link into a holy rhythm of life, to rest with God for a while.

❊ The Sabbath day is a balance issue. It is rightly promoted in health magazines as an antidote to stress and disintegration. But rest without God is distraction, for in God alone is a soul at rest. In Christ we find the rest that restores the whole person.

❊ The Sabbath day is a regeneration. Nature shows us the importance of rest for regeneration, a constant visual psalm about the wisdom of quality time in communion with God and with one another.

❊ The Sabbath day is a mealtime. We gather at the table of the world to celebrate the great communion of heaven and earth in Christ. Together we listen to the story and offer gifts and share the food and give thanks. It is a restoration time.

The Sense of Sunday

> To lose a sense of Sunday as the Lord's Day, a day to be sanctified, is symptomatic of the loss of an authentic sense of Christian freedom, the freedom of the children of God.
>
> *Sacramentum Caritatis*, 73

There was a coal mine in the town that had given jobs and prosperity to many generations of the townspeople. It had, over the years, taken on iconic status in the hearts of many – it was a family meeting place. The mine was closed down in the 1960s due to inadequate productivity, despite angry protests from the local workers. It was to be replaced with nuclear energy: cleaner, more productive and more attractive to foreign investors. The legal and government bodies worked assiduously to bring the new dream to birth with its promise of better wages, better working conditions and better market potential. Without much difficulty they acquired assistance from international banking systems and the secure financial base put the nuclear project on a firm footing. In addition the location of the plant on the ocean front was particularly attractive for shipping. Ten years later a terrible beauty was born!

The townspeople got new jobs and new housing and their wages increased – as did their mortgages and their grocery bills. The town soon became a city and the city became an international business centre. Other workers were shipped in to increase productivity and soon a highly structured system of work shifts was established. This would be a 24/7 operation, independent of dawn and dusk, of weekday and Sabbath day. The plant with its multiple reactors was a world wonder. It accelerated competition and intensified human effort.

As the years passed, the people grew tired of the monotony and they began to miss the meeting place. Their new up-market existence had become a bondage. They were exhausted with busyness. Soon the language of ancient Egypt began to be heard and words like 'slave labour' and 'let my people go' filled the coffee breaks. The people were very aware that living things need to breathe but they simply didn't have the time. It was the suggestion of Sabbath time that broke the deadlock, but the management said that the very notion was absurd. And the people bowed and prayed.

The change came more quickly than expected. It began with a rumbling in the earth, followed by a tidal wave never seen before. The great plant trembled and began to release its power. The people sought refuge in the coal mine and cried for their children and for their children's children.

Let Us Pray

Blessed be God.
Blessed be the holy name of God.
Blessed be the rhythm of God's work.
Blessed be the rest from labour.
Blessed be the song of rest in the plan of God.
Blessed be the hour of sunset.
Blessed be the Sabbath candle.
Blessed be the Sabbath prayer.
Blessed be the Sabbath heart.
Blessed be the worshipping people.
Blessed be the meeting place.
Blessed be the holy time.
Blessed be the eternal rest.

THE HOLY HOUR
LUKE 9:28-36

'NOW, ABOUT EIGHT DAYS AFTER THESE SAYINGS, JESUS TOOK WITH HIM PETER AND JOHN AND JAMES, AND WENT UP ON THE MOUNTAIN TO PRAY.' Prayer is the beginning of new things, a doorway to new visions. It is a decision to climb the mountain of discovery, to taste the breath of heaven and to see the shape of earth. We are going to the mountain top to the table of transfiguration, to see the New Jerusalem. It is a testing climb and the mountain of darkness casts its shadow on our slope, reminding us of a divine identity that is linked to a cross. The ascent carries us into the prayer space and in the dialogue time we await the glory of God.

'AND WHILE HE WAS PRAYING, THE APPEARANCE OF HIS FACE CHANGED, AND HIS CLOTHES BECAME DAZZLING WHITE.' He was in communion with God, lifting us up from the dust of the earth to shine like the sun. He was taking Peter, James and John, Moses and Elijah and all creation beyond historical time, into God's presence. The prayer intensified and became a turning point and we experienced the strength of climbers, holding on to the rope for the sake of others, for the vision from the top. Another mountain was now the place of Holy Communion, linking all creation, in its time and in its humanity, to the victory of the Lamb. The transformation was everywhere.

Moses and Elijah have returned to the mountain to witness the handover and to experience the fullness of their interpretation. Today prophecy itself is transfigured, for there is a new Moses leading a new exodus. In the new prophet, the person of God is visible, spreading the light from the mountain top over all the earth. Those who lift up their eyes in the mountain prayer will see the glory of the first light.

'Just as they were leaving him, Peter said to Jesus, "Master, it is good for us to be here; let us make three dwellings, one for you, one for Moses, and one for Elijah … "' It is good for us to have made the journey to the mountain top and seen a different view, to have witnessed the changing landscape and beheld the rising sun. It is good for us to have made the journey of prayer and heard the ancient story, to have woven the threads of history and watched the prophets adore. It is good for us to have made the journey of continuity and felt the burning bush, to have desired a mountain chapel and touched the face of God. It is good for us to have remembered the desert hut where God lived with us and to have burned with desire for another tent where we will live as one. It was good for us to have been transformed on the mountain of the covenant, ever ancient, ever new, changed in the light of the Lamb.

'While he was saying this a cloud overshadowed them; and they were terrified as they entered the cloud.' The mountain itself became the dwelling place and they who had come to the Tent of Meeting were drawn irresistibly into the great embrace. It covered them with the cloud of presence and led them into the tabernacle. They were afraid of the unknown experience but the purity of the Light wiped away their limitations and they fell to the ground, transfigured in the fullness of his presence. It was the Father who had named him at his Baptism, who is still calling forth his son to continue the journey that the people may listen. The voice from the cloud is putting the pieces together for us, for this is another mountain and a new Moses and the Torah now resides in him. Listen to him! On the mountain our very sigh is transfigured as the entire Scripture, its Law and its prophecy, is reflected through Jesus, the Christ, forevermore. This was the purpose of the ascent, the gift of the prayer time.

Homily Thoughts

❋ The Transfiguration is the fulfilment of history where the Old Testament and the New Testament achieve their full brilliance in Jesus.

❋ The Transfiguration is a visible sign of the Glory of God. It is truly a sacramental moment; God is present in the sign. The entire world is full of visible signs of God's presence. We need to stand in the prayer space in order to experience a different perspective, to experience the glory.

❋ The Transfiguration confirms the identity of Jesus. We see that the physical Jesus is indeed the One he claims to be. Here the divine and human natures have a single expression, namely, the Glory of God.

❋ The Transfiguration is about the exodus of all creation, through the flesh into glory. It confirms our hope of leaving the tomb and seeing the Light. As we give eyewitness to the glory of God in Jesus, and as we observe a human face shining like the sun, we are strengthened in our belief of a glorious body. Moses and Elijah are on the mountain, alive! Jesus is in glory. The apostles are astonished. We have entered the Resurrection time.

❋ The Transfiguration of Jesus reveals the meeting place of heaven and earth. The entire biblical journey is unveiled on the mountain and the cloud of Sinai has returned in the person of Jesus. God is here, in the flesh of Jesus and like the three disciples we also want to stay.

The Desire to Adore

> In the Eucharist, the Son of God comes to meet us and desires to become one with us. Eucharistic adoration is simply the natural consequence of the eucharistic celebration. The Act of Adoration outside of Mass prolongs and intensifies all that takes place during the liturgical celebration itself.
>
> *Sacramentum Caritatis, 66*

The chapel was silent in the afternoon sun and the prayer candles flickered with the memories they honoured. A lone woman kept vigil, motionless in the stilled atmosphere, waiting as she had promised. She had come on behalf of the parish to keep company with the mystery, to be there when he spoke, to receive what he offered. The woman saw herself as the keeper of the hospitality, the one who had come to welcome. She sat and watched him at the table, feeling his awareness, noticing how his presence deepened the space they shared. She lit another candle just to mark the moment.

His body had the shape of bread, reminding her of the Sunday meal when they had gathered in community for the blessing and the breaking, for the receiving and the sharing. Now in this chapel time, it had the fragility of the servant wanting to put things right, to receive the callers, to keep the memory of the table alive. The woman prayed that day for all who sat at table, at broken tables and at high tables, at family tables and at lonely tables. She asked him to move his presence to the silent tables and to the empty tables. She asked especially for his presence on the table of the world that all might taste the Bread of Life.

The light of the sun was lower now and the chapel reflected the merging lights. The flowers began to lower their heads and the sanctuary lamp brought up its flame.

The stained glass windows surrounded the sacred space and angel choirs sang 'Worthy is the Lamb'. The woman saw the transformation of the hour and how creation gathered for evening prayer. As the radiance of peace settled on the chapel air, the woman remembered the mountain top and she fell to the ground that she might adore.

LET US PRAY

Blessed be God.
Blessed be the holy name of God.
Blessed be the mountain, prayer of God.
Blessed be the light from the eyes of God.
Blessed be the transforming presence of God.
Blessed be the glory of God.
Blessed be the prophets of God.
Blessed be the cloud, shelter of God.
Blessed be the Chosen Son of God.
Blessed be Jesus, the radiance of God.
Blessed be Jesus, the tent of God.
Blessed be Jesus, the brilliance of God.
Blessed be Jesus, the revelation of God.

The Food of Life
John 6:27-59, 10:10

'Do not work for the food that perishes but for the food that endures for eternal life, which the Son of Man will give you.' Jesus could very well be addressing our culture of productivity and urging us to revise our understanding of 'the product'. He is cautioning us against intensifying our efforts in the cause of nothingness, whereby both effort and product will perish. The defining issue here is food, its quality and its purpose. If food is synonymous with life then this essential relationship must be rigorously protected by our choice of nutrients. Life is in the hope and in the promise, in the source and in the summit, and therefore we eat that we may become imperishable and so yield a harvest of rich fruit. This is the longing that awakened the prophets. Job dreamed of this achievement and so he searched the north and south, the east and west for God. David discovered that the Law of God was the food of his life – more precious than gold. Jeremiah understood that it was the Word of God that filled his heart with joy and happiness. Jesus' own response to the great hunger was to become the food that endures for eternal life.

'It was Moses who gave you the bread from heaven, but it is my Father who gives you the true bread from heaven.' The bread in the desert of Sinai sustained the people and deepened their understanding of a God who walks beside us. In the desert, bread and physical well-being became inseparable from bread and covenant relationship.

Forevermore Israel would remember God as the One who fed them with the manna of his abiding presence, the saving food of sustaining love, nurturing the body and deepening the covenant. This ancient memory broadens our context of the Bread of Life as that which nourishes every expression of life until life itself is filled with the fullness of God, in time and in eternity.

Without the 'true Bread' we cannot experience the real magnificence of life nor survive the desert crossing. It is imperishable food, a cosmic gift, the anointed flesh, the Lamb on the table, a love beyond all telling. Jesus Christ has become a meal-time issue! In a culture driven and shaped by food-related debates, the hunger deepens and the tables are folded. As we eat more, we want more and although satiated we remain dissatisfied. Jesus who came to take away hunger offers us the food that will transform us and fill our emptiness. He awaits us at the table.

'I am the bread of life. Whoever comes to me will never be hungry and whoever believes in me will never be thirsty.' There is an ache in the human heart, a search in the human brain, a pleading in the human spirit for food. Hunger is the abiding human call, our daily reach for completion. Although veiled in the robe of plenty, hunger still stalks the land and as material monuments dominate the global empire, with signposts pointing in the wrong direction – the thirst for something that satisfies intensifies. In this reality, food becomes the critical issue. It is the subject of our gatherings and the centre of our worship. It is the content of our memory and the sustenance of our journey. It is the experience of our celebrations and the inspiration of our shared stories. It is the passageway from here to eternity. In Christ, the food of life is the manna become the person, releasing us from captivity, feeding the starving multitude.

'This is indeed the will of my Father, that all who see the Son and believe in him may have eternal life;

AND I WILL RAISE THEM UP ON THE LAST DAY.' The will of God is for us to taste the food that will take us beyond the limits. From ancient Israel, life was understood as life with Yahweh. The One who at the beginning ordered chaos, had the single purpose of leading all creation to freedom. Abraham and Sarah understood this and Abraham built an altar to invoke the name of the One who promised the land. The prophets also envisioned life beyond the grave, when bodies would rise and dry bones would breathe again. God cannot be understood apart from life and the presence of Jesus in time is the ultimate testimony to this.

'I CAME THAT THEY MAY HAVE LIFE AND HAVE IT ABUNDANTLY.' Jesus sets himself before us as the one who is synonymous with the abundant life. He does not deal in small amounts and his eyes and his heart speak of plenty. From this abundance a river flows, rich in pardon, flavoured in Grace, fresh with living things. Food is now about the abundance of life in God and to eat the food of life is to find our place at the table of the Lamb. The food that does not perish is wrapped in love and prepared on the altar; it is shared in the Christian community and dispatched to the nations. This is the food that transforms human knowledge, changes outlooks and fills our consciousness. It has the quality of an infinite character and the abundance of overflowing generosity. It is the food of life.

HOMILY THOUGHTS

❋ There are many hungers in the human experience and satisfying hunger is a question of diagnosis and treatment. The hungers that rob us of life are the ones that take away our peace of mind and starve our emotional energy. Jesus is urging us to get in touch with the famine of the heart.

❧ The economic collapse of systems provides a useful insight into the famine of the heart and the way in which a reliance on perishables for nourishment makes for spiritual and moral bankruptcy.

❧ The food that Jesus is offering takes away hunger. It nourishes us into the fullness of life, where our eyes are open to discovery and our ears are alert to the cry of pain. The food of life strengthens the heart with hospitality and opens the hand with generosity. It is a food that nurtures gentleness and compassion and fills the body with the awareness of God.

❧ Perishable food has a short shelf life. Its 'use-by' date confirms its limited capacity. Jesus is asking us to consider searching for food that endures. This will be a journey of faith, a participation in a meal that will change our lives for ever. The food that endures to eternal life is freely given, available to all, non perishable. The one who believes this will never be hungry.

The Fullness of Life

> There is nothing authentically human – our thoughts and affections, our words and deeds – that does not find in the sacrament of the Eucharist the form it needs to be lived to the full.
>
> *Scaramentum Caritatis,* 71

He lived in the valley. It was inaccessible for eight months of the year as the treks and mountain passes gave way to the erosion of tropical rains and burst river banks. In the dry season he came out of his remote mission field and every day for four months, he drove his specially imported Dutch Jeep across miles of dirt roads, until he reached the city and got the supplies to keep the people alive when the clouds gathered. He bought medicines and food supplies, wood for the factory and sewing materials for the shop. There were the weightier items also, such as fertiliser for the maize fields, charcoal for the winter fires and bags of cement for general repair. His friends in Holland assisted in the replenishment and new vehicles were sent from home to keep open the bridge between life and death, between hope and despair.

The mission in the valley became the meeting place where hope was food and where home was community. The people danced in the evening time to welcome the food lorry and after the dawn Mass they sent Fr Dan on his way, back across the sun-dried earth, to find another load. Some people observed the relief effort as futile and non-productive. Others saw it as economically foolish and short-sighted.

The people in the valley, however, said that God had visited them and set them free. They had learned to live with the seasons and to negotiate with the rains. They had grown in their understanding of sharing and caring, of watching and waiting, of giving and depending. Especially, they had learned about food: how you can make enough for everyone and still return to the source in summertime for more. It was an abundant life in the valley, where the people lived as one and thanked God for Jesus Christ, who must have had a human heart like Fr Dan.

Let Us Pray

Blessed be God.
Blessed be the holy name of God.
Blessed be the fullness of life in God.
Blessed be Jesus, the food of God's life.
Blessed be Jesus, the food of eternal life.
Blessed be Jesus, the food of human hunger.
Blessed be Jesus, the food of human desire.
Blessed be Jesus, the food of human hope.
Blessed be the food that gathers the people.
Blessed be the food that transforms the gathering.
Blessed be the food that forms the community.
Blessed be the food that feeds the world.

The Cosmos On Fire
John 1:1-5, 14

'Before the world was created, the Word already existed; he was with God and he was the same as God.' The question about the identity of Jesus begins here, before the world began. We hold this moment of origin in ritual, song and story precisely because it is our story too. The identity of an entire universe rests on this single person, the Word who was with God, before time began. Through him and because of him we have come to know God and in him we continue to discover God. Though timeless, the Word became one of us and in flesh we beheld the closeness of God. He who is without beginning or ending revealed to us the nature of God and the nature of the people of God. He awakened in creation the hunger of the exile and the thirst of the desert nomad. When we came face to face with him we saw, in human form, a wonder never seen before and our hearts reached for the food of life.

'From the very beginning the Word was with God. Through him God made all things; not one thing in all creation was made without him.' It is simply not possible to be untouched by God, because just to be, is to be of God. Not one thing is without the design and depth of God. Not one thing is apart from God's anointing. It is by God's intense desire that all things took on form and began to breathe the breath of life. The Word, who was with God in the beginning, was the sign of God's intention to renew the face of the earth. He would bring the whole of creation with him, through the darkness, into the light. The Word bore in his being the glory of God, reminding us of the source, of the sacredness of all things, of our duty to relate all things to the Holy One. He spoke in small words and these became little lights and not one thing in all creation remained in darkness.

'THE WORD WAS THE SOURCE OF LIFE, AND THIS LIFE BROUGHT LIGHT TO MANKIND. THE LIGHT SHINES IN THE DARKNESS AND THE DARKNESS HAS NEVER PUT IT OUT.' He stood the light against the darkness to show what darkness can become, and yet he became the darkness that we might become the light. The difference between the places of darkness and light are clarified in him, with an eternal difference. He revealed how despair is the enemy of hope and how revenge is a death blow to forgiveness. He is our evidence that weakness is strength and that the trophy is not for the highest bidder. In this, the bravest of lights, we find the survival instinct that unravels the fear, dries the tears and opens the veil of darkness. Because he walked among us every bush is burning and every night is silenced by moonlight and starlight, by the yellow light of Venus and the stunning rings of Saturn. Because he walked among us the entire cosmos is reflecting light and men and women everywhere are lighting candles to announce the end of darkness. The baby cries after its night of labour, the puppy returns safely after the tsunami, the parcels of food fall from the aeroplane and the terror of the darkness passes and the light shines on.

'THE WORD BECAME A HUMAN BEING AND, FULL OF GRACE AND TRUTH, LIVED AMONG US. WE SAW HIS GLORY, THE GLORY WHICH HE RECEIVED AS THE FATHER'S ONLY SON.' In the Word, God – 'I am who I am' – expressed in human form the significance of this name as the revelation of history. God let go to desire and in the Son we saw a glory never seen before. As the Word emptied himself in the great act of giving birth to freedom, all creation was filled with the awareness of its source and the earth trembled with wonder. As the void yielded to God, the glory became a river of light, full of grace and truth, and the Word returned all things to their source. He was the self-revelation of God, the incarnation of the love in the covenant, and he lived among us. He amazed our senses when he entered our limited space and understanding, when he sat at our tables and broke bread with us. He amazed our expectation when he handed himself over and poured himself out to become food for the world. He fulfilled our deepest longings when he broke through death and abandoned the tomb. In a human person we saw the glory of God.

Homily Thoughts

- The story of Jesus begins in eternity. His family tree begins in God. John wants us to know that whatever is said about Jesus is said about God. Jesus is the only accurate information we have about God. John wants us to keep the nature of Jesus in mind as we travel through the Gospel. He wants us to know the author as well as the text.

- Jesus was with God in the beginning. When John recalls the opening words of Genesis we know that the full light of dawn is coming into the world. God is a personal being and this is the Light from on high.

- John is pointing to a new creation with the birth of Jesus in the flesh. This is the flesh that becomes the Bread of Life. When God became one of us, the Living Bread came down from heaven. It was the food that brought life to the world. It entered the darkness as an unquenchable light and because of this light darkness would never again prevail.

✤ Jesus is the victory over darkness. History itself is a testimony to the steadfast Light of the Word. Despite the shadows of Church and state which dim the Light, it still burns with an unbelievable intensity.

✤ Jesus stands both in eternity and in history and wherever Jesus is, the source of his origin flows in a living spring. Wherever Jesus is, God is, and John is making this point when he tells us that Jesus is full of truth and grace. The one who reveals God is Truth and the one who leads others to know God is the giver of grace.

The Great Light

> The Eucharist itself powerfully illuminates human history and the whole cosmos.
>
> *Sacramentum Caritatis*, 92

Something was unleashed in me as I watched the universe unfolding. I was one of the first stars called into light. Gradually the heavens became a fire and the growing light sent waves of awe and energy to the emerging creation. I soon became aware that the length and breadth and height and depth of light was beyond my grasp. The embryonic galaxies were trembling with wonder for they too had seen the light. Soon the seas and oceans and grasslands were joining the awareness and it seemed to me that all things visible and invisible were gathering around the table of light.

The primal sounds of the new creation became squeals of delight as they began to breathe out the light, and the stars sent out a river of starlight into the earth. As nature filled with abundance all around me and groaned in the great act of giving birth, I danced on the great arm of Jupiter just to mark the start of history. Already some stars were fading and others were being born but the source of the starlight was bubbling with fire. It had the shape of a human person, talking to other human persons, standing at the centre of this cosmic event. He was telling the writers of history about God.

As I listened to the dialogue, I learned about the opening in the void, of harmony in the heavens, of the One who was with God in the beginning. He was suffused in light from the beginning and as he breathed out the light of life, the darkness moved back and the earth began to feed off the sun and the people discovered bread in the land. It was the first sharing of bread that signalled into time a life that would endure, eternally. The Word, who brought heaven and earth together, opened our eyes to the knowledge of God's presence in the sparrows and the lilies, in the fig trees and growing seeds. Soon the whole cosmic order began to taste the bread of life and together the heavens and earth proclaimed the presence of God.

It was great to be a star in that beginning time and every time I twinkle with the light I do it with thanksgiving, for I too was with God in the beginning.

Let Us Pray

Blessed be God.
Blessed be the holy name of God.
Blessed be the desire of God in creation.
Blessed be Jesus, the Word of God made flesh.
Blessed be Jesus, the Word who is Light in the darkness.
Blessed be Jesus, the hope of all creation.
Blessed be Jesus, the centre of the glowing cosmos.
Blessed be Jesus, the glory of the heavenly lights.
Blessed be Jesus, the true manna from heaven.
Blessed be the universe, sacred arena of God's activity.
Blessed be the universe, giving and receiving the breath of God.
Blessed be the earth, home of the first Light.
Blessed be the earth, birthplace of the new creation.

THE DRINK OF WATER
JOHN 4:5-42

'IN SAMARIA HE CAME TO A TOWN NAMED SYCHAR. AND JESUS, TIRED OUT BY THE JOURNEY, SAT DOWN BY THE WELL. IT WAS ABOUT NOON.' What was a Jewish man doing in a Samaritan town? He knew the norms of racial prejudice and he knew what was said about men who associated with Samaritan women. This was not an accident of geography, but a decision of choice. Jesus will find us where we are, against all the odds, despite the threat of trial by public opinion. He will not be confined, neither will he be drawn into other people's analysis. With him, 'no-go' areas are link roads and lost sheep are the ones who have no water. It was about noon and the sun was warm with expectation as it brought together two weary travellers. Their common human thirst opened the conversation on life itself, and simple well talk became an exchange of feelings and insights, until the moment became an encounter and there was no going back. The Samaritan woman had tasted the living water and in a simple conversation of good will with the man from Galilee, they dismantled the historic wall of separation and joined hands to water the earth.

'A SAMARITAN WOMAN CAME TO DRAW WATER AND JESUS SAID TO HER, "GIVE ME A DRINK OF WATER."' Jesus opened the conversation; he took the initiative to begin the breakthrough. He was a stranger and the disadvantage was obvious to him. At best he was an object of suspicion, a possible threat in the neighbourhood, someone who could easily be reported to the security forces. His reputation had gone before him as the one who talked and laughed with children and embraced women. This was a moment of intense risk for Jesus of Nazareth. 'Give me a drink of water,' he said. The woman held her ground; she avoided the hearsay and went for the facts. She let the stranger speak and afforded him the courtesy of listening. It was the dignity of the man and the woman that put down a new marker when stranger meets stranger.

'THE WOMAN ANSWERED, "YOU ARE A JEW AND I AM A SAMARITAN – SO HOW CAN YOU ASK ME FOR A DRINK?"' How could I possibly have something to offer you? Are you actually saying that one man and one woman can begin the 'civilisation of love'? Do you really mean that with this worn and empty bucket I can carry living water? Surely you understand that if you drink from my bucket you will have ripped asunder the rock-solid division of the classes? Besides, if you share my vessel you will become unclean and that will lower your status forevermore. Do you not comprehend that the people with whom you associate may be seen by the stewards of the law as a blot on your personal record? So how can you dare to ask me for a drink?

'JESUS ANSWERED, "IF ONLY YOU KNEW WHAT GOD GIVES AND WHO IT IS THAT IS ASKING YOU FOR A DRINK, YOU WOULD ASK HIM, AND HE WOULD GIVE YOU LIFE-GIVING WATER."' If only you knew what is available to you, you would search for a deeper well. If only you knew, you would go with the river. If only you knew, you would leave your water jar and open your hands to the ocean. If only you knew, you would abandon the loneliness of Samaria and cross over into enemy territory. If only you knew, you would see in all women and in every rejected minority group a radiant light. If only you knew what I am offering you, the fear in your heart would give way to peace and your emptiness would become a living spring. If only you knew, your joy would awaken the village and your song would fill the earth. If only you knew, you would be fully alive.'

"'Sir," the woman said, "you haven't got a bucket and the well is deep. Where would you get that life-giving water?'" Water does not require a bucket. It takes its shape in the hospitality of the human heart. It is not for storing, but lives best where it moves and flows and spills over. It flows onward and outward and into and within, like an energy. Water is limitless in giving and abundant on its course. It forms channels of connection between peoples and places, and it enables currents of earth and sea to interact with the cosmic light. It is uncomfortable in bottles and bewildered on the supermarket shelf. Water loves accessibility and resists ownership of its source. It will not be defined by field nor pump, by economics nor profit gatherers. He didn't need a bucket that day, he was looking for the parched earth.

'Jesus answered, "Whoever drinks this water will be thirsty again but whoever drinks the water that I shall give will never be thirsty again.'" Jesus speaks to the woman of Samaria about a gift. It is a gift with a life connection. He is moving her focus beyond Jacob's well to the source of living water. The gift will ease her unrest and lead her to her moment of recognition. It will fill her and change her and transform her perspective on love. The gift he is offering will end the cravings of an unfulfilled life and lead her to the eternal spring. It will restore her awareness of her own dignity and awaken in her being the passion of the disciple. The well moment is the place of encounter, the ritual of gift giving. Enemy territory is no more and the gift is now available to friend and stranger, to Jew and gentile. The woman returned to the village and told the others to come out and taste the water.

Homily Thoughts

- The woman at the well reminds us that Jesus calls all of us to the waters of Baptism, to be changed for ever in his love. Baptism is the achievement of Jesus, our response to his invitation to drink living water.

- The woman at the well shows us that we too can be transformed if we listen to the words that Jesus speaks. The woman in Samaria allowed Jesus to engage with her; she listened and she responded, and once the dialogue was opened her life was never going to be the same again.

- The woman at the well teaches us about liturgy and how transformation happens for us where there is hospitality, acceptance and encounter.

- The woman at the well reveals to us the depths of Eucharist. She allows Jesus into her story and listens to his desire to be part of her life, to create a covenant with her, to turn things around for her. When Jesus offers to release her from thirst with the water of eternal life the woman pleads, 'Give me that water.'

- The woman at the well helps us to understand the importance of putting things right with family and friends in order to experience the fullness of Eucharist. She is the first person in John's Gospel to whom Jesus reveals his identity, 'I am he, I who am talking to you.' Jesus reveals himself to us when we come to the well.

- The woman at the well calls us to witness to what we have received and to tell the others that all the empty buckets will be filled.

THE WONDER OF THE GIFT

The wonder we experience at the gift God has made to us in Christ gives new impulse to our lives and commits us to becoming witnesses of his love.

Sacramentum Caritatis, 85

The teacher asked her senior class to write about gift giving and to think of the greatest gift they had ever received. There was one student who had lost both her parents in a plane crash and as she wrote about them she remembered very well all the wonderful things they had given her, right down to a substantial savings account when she reached her eighteenth birthday. But there was something else! They had been steadfast in their love for one another.

She remembered how they went to the park together to enjoy the grass and the trees. They always put aside time after Mass on Sundays for reading the newspapers and drinking hot chocolate. It was their unfailing respect, however, that lived most deeply in her memory, the kind of communication that says, 'I love you'. As she filled the pages of her notebook, the young student felt a palpable wonder at the sheer magnificence of her parents' relationship. It had become the bread of life for her, something that nourished her in good times and in dark times. It was the kind of love that spilled over into the neighbourhood and into the parish, just the way a well spills over with filling buckets. The love of her parents was the heart of every meal, that deepest joy in breaking bread together. Indeed, the young student remembered how mealtime in her parent's house was frequently shared with neighbours and friends, a lived experience of gift giving.

As she put her pen to paper that day the girl who had lost her parents felt strangely lucky! She had no inclination to write about gifts of gold and silver. Her legacy was of a different material. Her mother had loved her father and her father had loved her mother and now she was indeed the heiress and she knew that her bucket would spill over with the gift, forevermore.

Let Us Pray

Blessed be God.
Blessed be the holy name of God.
Blessed be the well of God's mercy.
Blessed be Jesus, true God and true man.
Blessed be Jesus, the spring of living water.
Blessed be Jesus, the gift of God's love.
Blessed be Jesus, who takes away our thirst.
Blessed be Jesus, who finds us in our emptiness.
Blessed be Jesus, who puts us together again.
Blessed be the woman who recognised him.
Blessed be the woman who became his disciple.
Blessed be the people who love like him.
Blessed be the Holy Spirit who leads us to the water.
Blessed be God in all people of good will.

THE SHARED GIFT
ACTS 2:42, 4:32-35

'THEY DEVOTED THEMSELVES TO THE APOSTLES' TEACHING AND TO THE FELLOWSHIP, TO THE BREAKING OF BREAD AND TO PRAYER.' The link between food and the story of God with us is woven through the biblical narrative. All major religions use food in their expressions of relationship with the Divine. At the Last Supper, Jesus shared his Body and Blood on the 'Table of the World' to complete the passing over of all creation, from death into life. When the early Christians met for the breaking of the bread, in the Word and in the meal, they knew that their liberation had been accomplished and they were now participants in the heavenly banquet. The image of a people gathered at table is the story of friendship. Tables are the places where stories are heard, where love is remembered and where food is shared. Tables are about presence and the quality of presence, our presence to one another and God's presence with us.

'THE GROUP OF BELIEVERS WAS ONE IN MIND AND HEART.' This was a radically new ethic, a different kind of gathering. The emerging Christian identity would be visible in the way people lived and loved together. By communion they would know themselves and become known to others. It was a blueprint that would never be erased, a testimony to the power of non-violence and responsible stewardship. With their collective vision, common faith and shared mission, the small group kept the dangerous memory of Jesus alive. Their code of hospitality expressed their communion with God and with one another, and many new converts were drawn to this group of people that loved one another. In the early Church, Eucharist was not merely a liturgical remembering but an essential relationship, a quality of hospitality, a Christ presence. By their very lives, the first Christian communities challenged the promises of consumerism and materialism and their prophetic voice continues to transform human minds and hearts in every generation, to the ends of the earth.

'No one said that any of his belongings were his own, but they all shared with one another everything they had.' The Church – the Body of Christ – exists for communion and to be a member of this unity is to be available as bread, broken and shared, for all the world. Receiving the Eucharist always implies a heart that is pledged to alleviate hunger, for communion with God cannot be achieved apart from communion with each other and with all creation. Holy Communion is the promise of a restored creation in the flesh of Jesus Christ, and participation in the eucharistic meal, therefore, is a partaking in Jesus' mission to set the downtrodden free. History has shown us that people of the Eucharist have alleviated the darkness in the lives of millions of people who subsist in the silent places of poverty. Pope Benedict has reminded us in *Sacramentum Caritatis* that eucharistic people have a 'service of charity', a pledge to look at all people with the 'perspective' of Christ.

'There was no one in the group who was in need. Those who owned fields or houses would sell them ... and the money was distributed to each one according to his need.' The theme of communion which defines Christian identity is the subject matter of the Christian mission. The great challenge of the Church's work in every age is to stand in society as a communion of people, bringing together, reconciling, extending the hand of friendship, breaking the bread, sharing the meal. Catholic social teaching repeatedly applies a theology of Eucharist to contemporary cultural values and asks all people to lend a helping hand in building a world in harmony with God's desire for communion. It was St John Chrysostom (386–397 AD) who reminded us that the One who said 'This is my Body' is the same One who said 'You saw me hungry and you gave me food.'

As we prepare for the 50th International Eucharistic Congress we tell again of the one man who died to set us free. This is a time of connection for every tribe and tongue and people and nation, baptised and unbaptised. Communion with Christ and with one another calls all creation to the 'civilisation of love'.

Homily Thoughts

- Eucharist is a global ethic. It is the steadfast hope of a world wrestling with the darkness of consumerism and individualism.

- Eucharist is a cosmic light. It is the way out of system failures and institutionalised blockages.

- Eucharist is the cry of the earth. It is the food of regeneration and the sustenance of every ecosystem.

- Eucharist is the pulse of the human heart. It is the rhythm of life, the breathing in and the breathing out.

- Eucharist is the communion of the people. It is the song of friendship, the dance of life.

- Eucharist is the awareness of poverty, the response of the listening ear. It is a shared resource.

- Eucharist is the message of the Word, the memory of the covenant. It is the worship of people.
- Eucharist is the gift of the Lamb, the Food of Life on the table of the world. It is the Body and Blood of Jesus Christ.

The Shared Gift

> The love that we celebrate in the sacrament is not something we can keep to ourselves. By its very nature it demands to be shared with all.
>
> *Sacramentum Caritatis*, 84

A single seed slipped from the cardboard package and fell on the garden path. The raindrops washed the seed into the front lawn and the soil, noticing how cold the fragile seed had become, it provided warmth and security to nurture the embryonic life. As the soil softened in the early summer rains, the seed sank contentedly into its protection and as it swelled with new life it began to move upward and outward. The soil was generous with its nutrients as it rooted the emerging life with stability and with confidence. When the fragile stem broke into the sunlight it was welcomed by a warm and intense energy.

The sun taught the infant stem how they could work together to produce leaves, then blossoms and then the very food of life. Soon the seed was opening its buds and new seeds were falling to the earth and the wind and the birds and the raindrops and gravity itself moved in to activate a dispersion system. There were seeds everywhere and the entire garden ecosystem was at full capacity, spreading life on the lawn, in the hedges and beyond the boundary walls. It was a commitment to sustainability and some insects were flat out, shredding organic matter for much needed compost and even giving their lives for the common good.

The fruit came in time for the harvest and the seed who started it all smiled with great delight. Now the humans could share the achievement and the entire garden community would be able to eat together. While they were at table the seed remembered the day that it fell from the cardboard packet and became one with the creatures of earth. It remembered how falling to earth was at first traumatic but how, in time, it had managed to forge a deep and lasting relationship with all things, living and non-living. Now, as they shared the fruits of their labour, all who participated in the meal were amazed at the possibility in one single seed. They had learned that bread is the gift for those who work together in the spreading of the seed.

Let Us Pray

Blessed be God.
Blessed be the holy name of God.
Blessed be the communion of God.
Blessed be Jesus, who became one with us.
Blessed be Jesus, who took us into his heart.
Blessed be Jesus, who gave us the Bread of Life.
Blessed be Jesus, who showed us the way of communion.
Blessed be Jesus, who reconciled the world to God.
Blessed be the people who have the mind and heart of Jesus Christ.
Blessed be the people who build up and restore friendship.
Blessed be the communion of saints, on earth and in heaven.
Blessed be God's love in the heart of the universe.

WHAT IS TRUTH?
JOHN 8:32, 18:37

'IF YOU HOLD TO MY TEACHING, YOU ARE REALLY MY DISCIPLES. THEN YOU WILL KNOW THE TRUTH AND THE TRUTH WILL SET YOU FREE.' The quest for truth is the driving theme in every biography, and stories of truth dismissed and ignored make for the escape routes in the human drama. The era of the Celtic Tiger in Ireland, with its false promise and blinkered assessments, has revealed how easily denial replaces reality and how easily fiction becomes fact. Jesus identified this snare as early as the first century of the Christian era, when he taught his disciples the importance of connecting with the source of life for the discovery of Truth. He pointed to himself as the one who is Truth – recognisable and eternal – the ultimate reality, the one who will set us free. Truth always guarantees release from bondage.

In recent times, Pope Benedict has returned many times to the topic of truth, reminding us on his eighty-fourth birthday that a life without truth is a life that passes us by. Without truth to guide us, we find ourselves yielding to the dominant voice or to the easiest option. Without truth, all is relative and life itself is adrift. The pursuit of truth is not just a Christian ideal, it is a universal responsibility. The Pope urges us to return to Jesus Christ as the food of truth in history, the one who is ever powerful without having any power.

'IN FACT, THE REASON I WAS BORN AND CAME INTO THE WORLD IS TO TESTIFY TO THE TRUTH. EVERYONE ON THE SIDE OF TRUTH LISTENS TO ME.' Although he was looking truth in the face, Pilate failed to recognise it. He was worried about a potential threat to Rome and the collapse of the institution. But in Jesus, truth had come before Pilate and the established order was indeed about to tremble. Pilate looked to the popular press and to the mob mentality to find his way forward. Worse still, he was overwhelmed by the power of the institution, so great that its own membership had disavowed their religious heritage – 'We have no king but Caesar' – to bring about the crucifixion of truth. Pilate was unable to listen to himself and to act in accordance with his own deepest knowledge that the man before him was innocent. He was another victim of relativism and pragmatism.

The Roman governor helps us to explore that place where something is real, irrespective of opinions to the contrary, however compelling these may be. In the presence of Jesus and Pilate, truth is clarified. It is not the subject matter of perception nor cultural emphasis; neither is it credentialed by majority vote. Truth is not the victim of tolerance, for a tolerance not built on truth is, in fact, intolerance. As Shakespeare once said, 'Truth is truth to the end of reckoning.'

Pilate's question is our question too. For the entire course of human history we have been trying to answer it: 'What is truth?' The question is still the food of civilisations, as power systems and law makers threaten to starve our consciousness of all suggestions of an eternal truth. When Jesus stood before Pilate and proclaimed that his teaching is the true testimony, he negated the philosophies that make everything true! He was explaining to Pilate the difference between the facts and the opinions, the reality and the interpretation, the text and the teacher. He knew very well that he would pay the price for this clarification of reality but he willingly went to the cross that we might understand the food of truth.

Homily Thoughts

✤ Truth is not neutral nor is it served by neutrality.

✤ Truth calls to us for a personal response: 'Everyone who is of the Truth listens to me.'

✤ Truth is always an invitation, as it was to Pilate; it is about choice and decisions.

✤ In the Gospel context, Truth is crucified by its own defenders!

✤ Truth asked Pilate to break with Rome. For many of us that is unimaginable.

✤ It is possible to have a trial where neither the accusers nor the judge respect the Truth. Sometimes it is the 'criminal' who holds the Truth.

✤ Truth makes power look foolish and power crucifies the Truth.

The Food of Truth

> In this Sacrament the Lord truly becomes food for us, to satisfy our hunger for truth and freedom. Since only the truth can make us free (cf. Jn 8:32), Christ becomes for us the food of truth.
>
> *Sacramentum Caritatis, 2*

Ireland has a long history of struggle for freedom. In the time of St Patrick (432 AD) the people were controlled by druids whose magical powers created terror in people's minds. Tara, the seat of kings and the political capital of Ireland, was the centre of druidism in the Ireland of Patrick's time. Before Rome, Tara, with its ancient civilisation, was a city of might in the western world and seemed destined to last for ever. The Royal House, however, had one major obstacle to overcome; it had to do battle with an eternal truth of irreversible magnificence. When Patrick entered this island with the Light of Christ, the power of Tara trembled.

It was Easter 433 when fires blazed on two hills of ancient Ireland and Slane and Tara faced the rising sun. The High King, Laoghaire, was enraged that someone would dare to light a fire before the traditional lighting of the great fire of Tara, the fire of kings. As Pilate turned to the chief priests and elders, Laoghaire turned to his druids for a solution to the rival fire. The druids were the judges, prophets and teachers of the time and they warned the king of the potential of Patrick's fire and how, if unquenched, it would spread and devour all other fires and even overthrow the power of Tara itself. It would have to be extinguished, quickly.

Patrick was brought to trial on Easter day. The two men, Laoghaire and Patrick, came face to face in the great banquet hall of Tara, the venue of festival and feasting, of legal trials and of religious rituals. It was the meeting of the great powers and the king listened as Patrick, without armour or army, explained that his fire was the fire of truth. Like Pilate before him, Laoghaire recognised the innocence of Patrick and he released the prisoner back to his own people. The meeting of the kingdoms marked a turning point in Irish history.

The challenge to Tara is symbolised in the lighting of the Paschal fire on the nearby Hill of Slane. When, on the eve of Easter 433, Patrick lit the fire of the resurrection on the territory of kings, the truth of Christ began to burn its way into the soul of Ireland, turning every hilltop into a burning bush and setting the druids free. Tara had burned itself out. It taught us that systems cannot be kindled at the expense of truth. The pride of former days was put to sleep!

LET US PRAY

Blessed be God.
Blessed be the holy name of God.
Blessed be the truth revealed by God.
Blessed be Jesus, true God and true man.
Blessed be Jesus, true splendour of God.
Blessed be Jesus, the Way, the Truth and the Life.
Blessed be all people who search for the Truth.
Blessed be all people who listen to the Truth.
Blessed be all people who recognise the Truth.
Blessed be all people who follow the Truth.
Blessed be the Holy Spirit who guides us in the Truth.
Blessed be the eternal Truth in time and in eternity.

THE ACCEPTANCE
MATTHEW 26:36-46

'THEN JESUS WENT WITH HIS DISCIPLES TO A PLACE CALLED GETHSEMANE.' It is a garden known to all people, in reality or in metaphor. Gethsemane is a place of intense loneliness and of extraordinary inner strength. The garden of shadows is always a deciding point and continuing on takes all our faith and all our courage. Giant olive trees remind us of survival in every season and in the shade of their great branches we seek shelter from the silence. The Passover moon is full and it is holding the light for us in the darkest hour, a faithful spotlight in this defining moment of life's journey. We remember the Garden of Eden and the unfaithfulness that broke the communion, but now in another garden Jesus has joined us for the final test and with him we will hold on to love.

'SIT HERE WHILE I GO OVER THERE AND PRAY.' Prayer is the only thing that can hold us together in Gethsemane. It is the steadfast anchor in the hour of suffering. Jesus was facing the horror of Roman crucifixion. He, a wholly good man is bewildered by human cruelty. Like us, he also wondered, 'What have I done?' As he collapses beneath the terror of the night he sees the secrets of the olive tree, carved on wood, enduring through generations. So Jesus prayed on the night he was betrayed. He prayed as he never prayed before, for escape and then for the holiness of those who hold on to love. In prayer he found companionship, the presence of angels, the arms of God. The world waited! He decided to go on, to be the redemptive gift, to forgive the debt of selfishness. He would become the bailout on the table of the world. Because of Gethsemane we are never alone when the storm clouds rage against us.

'The sorrow in my heart is so great that it almost crushes me.' Give us strength for the last mile! At some level, agony is always experienced alone. The sorrow comes over us and we stumble into absence. He was crushed by his failed effort and by his aborted plan. He was crushed by his failure in friendship and his broken relationship with Judas. He was crushed by the volatility of Peter and by the uncertainty of those who abandoned him. He was crushed by the blindness of the institution and by the politics of leadership. He had come to this place to walk a mile in our shoes, to fulfil the dream of communion but the sorrow in his heart nearly turned him back. He looked to his friends for support but they were sleeping and so he faced the final ascent alone, to hand over his body that the heart of the universe might go on beating.

'Stay here and keep watch with me.' Gethsemane, the garden he loved so well, where he frequently went to pray, now asks so much of him. Gethsemane, the garden where he found stillness and strength so many times, now asks for his life. The places we love do that; they ask us to leave and pass on. Jesus needed someone to witness to this moment of decision, people who would see first hand the meeting of love and sacrifice, where the cost is not counted and a life is handed over. We will stay awake with him and be the eyewitnesses. We will write it on our hearts and remember it in our wounds. Together we will face the final ascent under the weight of the wood.

'My Father, if it is possible, take this cup of suffering from me! Yet, not what I want but what you want.' It is very difficult to say the words, 'Thy will be done.' Acknowledging what is over is difficult to do. The very acceptance plunges us into immense sadness. The words throb with memories, deep with raw human emotion. The Kedron valley stands in disbelief as Jesus rolls in the anguish of the false kiss that rejects his love. But he will drink the cup and take the blows and vanquish death until the last sheep makes it through Gethsemane. Take Lord, receive all that I possess, for this I came into the world, to cross over, to become the Bread. My destiny is through the garden.

I will kneel where Jesus knelt. It will give me strength for a love that goes to the end. I adore the love that did not refuse the final hour. I adore the love that stands beside me in the shadows. I adore the love that held on for me. He aligned his will to the will of God, perfectly. Now I understand love and I am free.

HOMILY THOUGHTS

❧ Gethsemane is the place where death and resurrection do battle. The garden itself, in its seasons, reminds us that nothing dies but something lives. Gethsemane always asks us to wait it out until springtime comes.

❧ Gethsemane is the place of the struggle that turned into victory. The victory of Gethsemane is the knowledge of our faith and the strength that faith awakens in us to survive the darkness until the dawn breaks.

❧ Gethsemane is the place where Jesus is present, writhing in our pain, standing beside us under the olive tree. It may take us to the brink of ruin, rob us of our friends, shut down our livelihood, still we will not be overcome because we are never alone in Gethsemane.

❊ Gethsemane is the place of the ultimate generosity of love. Jesus abandoned his will to the will of God, for the common good, for all creation. Discipleship will always be a journey through the garden for the sake of the nations, because of love.

A LOVE WHICH GOES TO THE END

> What more could Jesus have done for us? Truly, in the Eucharist he shows us a love which goes 'to the end', a love which knows no measure.
>
> John Paul II, *Ecclesia de Eucharistia*, 11

It was a birthday celebration. Teresa was forty and her parents had planned something really special. Teresa herself had some awareness of the occasion, especially the promise of a birthday cake. She had a rather restless night of expectation and when her mother brought the orange juice, as she had done for all the other days to herald the time of awakening, Teresa was unresponsive.

Bridie called Tommy, just to get a second opinion and both parents knew as they held the orange juice that Teresa would not make it to her birthday party. Bridie whispered to Tommy, 'God's will be done.' And Tommy remembered how he himself had said the very same words the first day he held baby Teresa, forty years ago.

It had been a long journey for parents and child. Some people said that Bridie and Tommy were 'doing their Gethsemane'. Others regretted how two young people were forced to put their lives on hold for forty years. The parents themselves took a different view. Teresa was the gift that they had been given and she was theirs to have and to hold until the night passed. The neighbours and extended family helped. They helped with watching and waiting and Bridie and Tommy understood when at times they got tired and left. The hours of every day became their sacred ritual as they ministered to the wounded one and nourished her in the food of their love.

It was a grinding schedule and sometimes their love was brought to the ground and their anguish threatened their dedication. They experienced the betrayal of systems and the abandonment of promises. They learned many times about dashed hopes and failed dreams. At times they had known the unbearable fatigue of monotony and the numbed feeling of those who are nailed to a cross. But they had never given up! Love held them together and anointed their work and made their hearts like unto God's. They laid down their lives as he had once done, with the magnificence of the love outright. When Bridie said her final 'Thy will be done' on the morning of Teresa's fortieth birthday she knew that she and Tommy were part of a great redemptive story for the life of the world.

LET US PRAY

Blessed be God.
Blessed be the holy name of God.
Blessed be the steadfast love of God.
Blessed be Jesus Christ, the Word of God made flesh.
Blessed be Jesus in the Garden of Gethsemane.
Blessed be Jesus, whose love overcame the darkness.
Blessed be Jesus, who suffered intensely for us.
Blessed be Jesus, who accepted God's will.
Blessed be Jesus, who gave us everything he had to give.
Blessed be Jesus, whose love endured to the finish.
Blessed be all people who keep company with Jesus in Gethsemane.

Blessed be the Light of Christ that goes before us in the night
of suffering.
Blessed be all people who never give up on love.

THE ALTAR OF THE WORLD
JOHN 13:1-10

'JESUS KNEW THAT HIS HOUR HAD COME FOR HIM TO LEAVE THIS WORLD AND GO TO THE FATHER ...' So he got up from the meal. Took off his outer clothing and wrapped a towel around his waist. He took off his outer garment, something he would do again at the final hour. He was letting go to the ultimate sacrifice, handing over his life with a towel. The garment was in the way of what he wanted to do; it was restricting his body and shielding his real identity, for he was really the servant king, a Messiah without power. The people at table with him on that Passover night had not offered to wash the feet. They had missed the moment of hospitality. This ritual of reception and of cleansing was integral to the communion at table and its omission denied the purpose of the gathering. Jesus, feeling the desire for a sign of love and friendship, reached for the basin and towel.

'AFTER THAT HE POURED WATER INTO A BASIN AND BEGAN TO WASH HIS DISCIPLES' FEET, DRYING THEM WITH THE TOWEL THAT WAS WRAPPED AROUND HIM.' Washing feet was a way of greeting since at least the time of Abraham (Gen 18:4). It was a gesture of welcome for the guest, a relief from the fatigue of the journey. The lowliest servant usually did the feet washing, although the action itself was very significant. In offering one's feet for washing, the guest knew that the journey was over and the 'welcome home' had begun.

'HE CAME TO SIMON PETER, WHO SAID TO HIM, "LORD, ARE YOU GOING TO WASH MY FEET?" JESUS REPLIED, "YOU DO

NOT REALISE NOW WHAT I AM DOING, BUT LATER YOU WILL UNDERSTAND.'" You will understand that Communion gives us a language to dialogue with every tongue. You will understand that washing feet is a way of being in the world; it is a mandate from the table to shape a Eucharistic culture. No one can give Eucharist if that person does not first receive it and no one has received Eucharist unless one is transformed by it. Peter is faced with a life-altering decision. A Eucharistic life, in every time and place, is available to love. It gives witness to the seamless connection between communion with God and with one another and it is ever available for the washing of the feet.

"'No,' SAID PETER, "YOU SHALL NEVER WASH MY FEET." JESUS ANSWERED, "UNLESS I WASH YOU, YOU HAVE NO PART WITH ME.'" It is a moment when love is asking to be received, accepted. It requires the intimacy of absolute trust and the humility of absolute need. Giving is easier and Peter knows that. He knows that life is more secure and predictable when no one rocks the institution. It is unthinkable, unacceptable even, for the leader to turn things around, to reverse the roles and take off the garment of office. Peter is now faced with the question of giving over his feet – dirty and tired, worn and travelled. If he gives them over to be washed he will be forming a communion, yielding to the invitation, participant in the new world order. With all his strength Peter tries to stop the clock and prevent the earthquake, but the hour has come and Jesus needs people who will let go the grime and dust of closed roads. 'Not only my feet ... '

'I HAVE SET YOU AN EXAMPLE THAT YOU SHOULD DO AS I HAVE DONE FOR YOU.' We are moving deeper into the character of Christ. He is a leader who performs tasks that no one else will do. He works his way through the barrier of cultural expectation and reverses the custom. As we observe him with the towel and basin we learn that every gesture of washing away the scars of the journey is indeed a 'washing of feet'. As we see him bathe the wounds, we see that Christianity, from its beginning, has meant a network of relationships, a web of life sustained by the Bread on the altar of the world. He who worked tirelessly for a 'civilisation of love' now girds himself with a towel, that we too may understand service and give our bodies to heal the wounds of war and hatred and to build the bridge of communion. Washing feet is forevermore the place of meeting and of going forth. While they were at table he gave them bread for receiving and for going forth.

Homily Thoughts

❄ The towel and the basin remind us that service is always about someone else. It is an action that notices the need and tries to relieve it. Service takes us into the reality of the other person; it is about changing places.

❄ The service of Jesus makes us feel better. It gives us a sense of being welcomed, of belonging. When Jesus knelt down beside us he saw the blisters and pain of the journey and he washed away the soreness. With a basin and towel he raised us up.

❄ The service of Jesus is a challenge to our economic structure. Free gifts do not fit the market ethic of our time. Like Peter we find it difficult to comprehend a gift of this magnitude, a love that stands in for us and stands up for us and kneels down for us.

❄ The towel and basin set a new standard for leadership. As symbols of office they represent a way of leading at ground level.

THE ALTAR OF THE WORLD

> Even when it is celebrated on the humble altar of a
> country church, the Eucharist is always in some way
> celebrated on the altar of the world.
>
> *Ecclesia de Eucharistia*, Introduction

It was Thursday, a wet evening at the end of summer, the
twenty-first day of August, 1879. Times were difficult in
Ireland and evictions, famines and sickness plagued the land.
Into this place of desolation, a light of eternal brilliance was
about to shine.

Mary McLoughlin was the first to notice the mysterious
light on the south wall of the parish church in Knock, Co.
Mayo. She called her friend, Mary Byrne, and the two women
were the first witnesses to an event of heavenly proportion.
The news brought out the neighbours, and the small group
– ranging in age from six-year-old John Curry to seventy-five-
year-old Bridget Trench – became agents in the communion
of heaven and earth. They stood in the rain that evening,
gazing, astonished. Before them, on the gable wall they beheld
an amazing vision. Mary was there, with Joseph and John
the evangelist. They were keeping company with the Lamb,
vulnerable and alone, on the altar of the world. The cross
beside him was empty, for he had paid the ultimate price and
now as he gathered the family in rural Ireland, his gift was the
victory of resurrection.

The angels were also there, witnessing to the moment
when heaven became visible in County Mayo. There were no
words spoken in Knock that evening. As the group became
fully conscious participators in a mystery beyond all telling,
they were filled with silence.

Mary herself was silent for she knew that the altar of sacrifice
was the message. With her whole body she was drawing the
gathering to the altar. John the evangelist held an open Bible

which focussed the liturgical gathering on the Word, the One who became bread for the world. Joseph bowed his head in silent adoration.

The message of Knock is the liturgy of heaven and earth, the cosmic event that gathers angels and saints, men, women and children at the banquet table.

In 1979, Blessed John Paul II made a personal pilgrimage to Knock Shrine and as he knelt at the gable wall one felt that the golden rose had blossomed. The vision entrusted to the people for so long was now blessed by Rome. It is estimated today that one and a half million people visit Knock Shrine annually. It is the meeting place of the nations, seeking shelter, needing healing, longing for peace. Knock Shrine is indeed a table for the world.

LET US PRAY

Blessed be God.
Blessed be the holy name of God.
Blessed be the closeness of God.
Blessed be Jesus, true God and true man.
Blessed be Jesus on the altar of the world.
Blessed be Jesus, Bread of angels and of all humanity.
Blessed be Mary, mother of God.
Blessed be Mary, Lady of Knock, Queen of Ireland.
Blessed be St Joseph, guardian of the family.
Blessed be St John, teacher of the Word.
Blessed be the men, women and children who saw the light.
Blessed be the angels who came to Mayo.
Blessed be all who worship at the table of the Lamb.

A Woman of the Eucharist
Luke 1:26-38

'In the sixth month of Elizabeth's pregnancy, God sent the angel Gabriel to Nazareth, a town in Galilee, to a virgin pledged to be married to a man named Joseph, a descendant of David. The virgin's name was Mary.' The return of Gabriel (cf. Dan 8:16; 9:21) marks the dawn of a new age and in receiving the news Mary moves human history to its hour of glory. God has remembered. The transformation begins in Nazareth, the ordinary place. Nazareth provides the place where heaven and earth can join in praise. Mary is the collaborator in the divine plan of salvation, the favoured one, for she too has remembered. She has remembered the writings of the prophets and the story of her ancestors. She knows that at every age, God called people to radical participation in the plan of salvation. The unfolding of God's presence was always in collaboration with us. God's love for us is now interwoven with Mary's love, and from this unique personal relationship, Mary gives us an insight into the transforming power of the love that has come to visit us. Jesus will feed the hungry with good things and sustain the lowly ones. He will bring down oppressive systems and reverse accepted social structures. His entrance into our flesh is the dawn of a new perspective and with mercy he will begin the great restoration.

Forevermore the name of Mary will be inseparable from her son, the Messiah, for she has formed a meeting place for the Old and the New Covenants. In human terms, Mary unveils what God has promised for all creation since the beginning of time, and as her dialogue with heaven opens, all creation is called to rejoice.

'YOU WILL CONCEIVE AND GIVE BIRTH TO A SON, AND YOU ARE TO CALL HIM JESUS. HE WILL BE GREAT AND WILL BE CALLED THE SON OF THE MOST HIGH.' This is the announcement that all creation has been groaning for. It fulfils God's promise to send a redeemer (Gen 3:15). From the dust of the earth, from the oppression in Egypt, from the exile with strangers, the people have thirsted for this breakthrough. It is the holy communion, the day of restoration. Because of Mary we understand 'tabernacle' as the space of the heart where Jesus finds a dwelling place; the house where the people gather. In focussing the presence of God for us, Mary draws us into the many places where God is manifested in our time. She takes us back to the ordinary, to the quiet service, to the gift that doesn't count the cost. Through Mary we learn more deeply that Eucharist is an action of God, unique and irreversible, offering unimagined possibilities for all creation.

"'I AM THE LORD'S SERVANT," MARY ANSWERED. "MAY YOUR WORD TO ME BE FULFILLED."' This is the dialogue that began the reconciliation of the world to God. Mary's faith remained unshakable even when she was asked to take an unknown road and to risk the price of ridicule. When the woman responds to the angel we begin to grasp that Eucharist is a giant leap for the giver and the receiver, the seal of the covenant. When she offered her will to the divine plan, Mary initiated for us the great Eucharistic welcome, the hospitality of the person, filled with grace. With her son, Mary has become the hope of Israel. She who received the Son of God into her body, into time, into the story of humanity, must give answer. She will become the woman of the Eucharist, a servant of God in word and in deed, an apostle to the nations, a mother to the world. At Mary's consent God unites his divinity with the human condition and her acceptance is the faith of the servant who is available on the table of the world. She is now the God-bearer, the woman of the Eucharist.

HOMILY THOUGHTS

❧ Mary said 'Amen' to the Word made flesh. It was the first Eucharistic moment. Since then we have re-echoed this great Amen to the presence of God-with-us through the humanity of Jesus.

❧ Mary received the body of Christ. She was told of his identity and she believed. Mary's faith is instrumental in the story of our salvation. It is faith that opens to us the nearness of God.

❧ Mary offered her body as a dwelling place for Christ. In this she became a channel of God's love in history, a meeting place for heaven and earth, a liturgical centre.

❧ Mary announced the transforming power of Christ with us, the new world order that would be achieved in Christ and the hunger that would be filled.

❧ Mary hosted the first Eucharistic gathering in Bethlehem where the people assembled to tell the story, to offer gifts and to give thanks.

❧ Mary was there at the hour of darkness, staying with him through the final hour. The Woman of the Eucharist took his cross to herself and became the Mother of the Church.

Star of the Sea

> Above all let us listen to Mary Most Holy, in whom the
> mystery of the Eucharist appears, more than in anyone
> else, as a mystery of light.
>
> *Ecclesia de Eucharistia*, 62

The title 'Star of the Sea', attributed to St Jerome, is a much
loved name for Mary, mother of God. Some ancient Christian
hymns and prayers inspired by this title have stood the test
of time. When we reflect on Mary's role in the story of God-
with-us, the imagery of the star is particularly appropriate.
We remember that in the beginning, God put the stars in the
sky for the purpose of lighting the earth and to separate light
from darkness (Gen 1:16-17). The star also links us back to the
Star of David, to our ancient past, to the line of salvation. In
our time, the art of horoscope reading is eagerly celebrated by
many people, emphasising our hunger for a guide, something
we can depend on to accompany us on life's journey. These
twinkling lights then, deeply woven into our story and into
our imagination, keep watch with us on the breath of heaven.
They are not afraid of the journey that takes them into the
night, nor do they escape the terror of darkness. They are
resilient in the silent time until the morning breaks. When
we address Mary as 'Star' we know that we are standing in the
light of a star of great brilliance.

The navigators of former times depended on the stars to
lead them through the night. As they steered by the stars
they were confident that they were moving into the dawn.
The North Star in particular was the traveller's friend, their
faithful companion when they lost sight of the land and
pushed out into the ocean. The image of the star as the light
of safety and protection may have its origin with the pagan
goddess, Isis, who originated in the sea and was believed to
be the protector of seafarers. When we pray, therefore, with

Mary, Star of the Sea, we evoke all the symbolism of the star as the one who reflects the Great Light and guides us on our journey into the morning.

The star symbolism reflects the light which Mary shone in the universe. Pope Benedict, in his second encyclical, *Spe Salvi* ('in hope we are saved'), explains this light as the 'Star of Hope'. Like the cloud above the sea (1 Kgs 18:41-45), Mary also heralded the ending of a long drought and the beginning of the great feast. In truth, she is the one who gave flesh to Jesus Christ and now all generations call her blessed, the Woman of the Eucharist, the mother who leads us to the table.

LET US PRAY

Blessed be God.
Blessed be the holy name of God.
Blessed be Jesus, the son of God and son of Mary.
Blessed be Jesus, who came to live in Nazareth.
Blessed be Jesus, who learned from Mary and Joseph.
Blessed be Mary, who received the angel Gabriel.
Blessed be Mary, who welcomed God's invitation.
Blessed be Mary, mother of Jesus and woman of the Eucharist.
Blessed be all people who long for the Bread of Life.
Blessed be all people who eat at the table of the Lord.
Blessed be the angels who celebrate the Eucharist with us.
Blessed be the gift that sets us free.